BASIC ROCK CLIMBING

Bouldering, Crack Climbing and General Rock Climbing Techniques

Sam Fury

Illustrations by Shumona Mallick

Dedications

Amanda Mckenna

Cyrus Hands

Debbie Herbert

Karthi Mcloed

Jamie Bennet

Steve Winslow

Safety Note

Do not practice rock climbing without proper equipment and safety training.

Any reputable rock climbing gym will give you the necessary safety instruction needed to practice climbing safely. Take advantage of it

The information found in this publication is for training and/or reference purposes only. It is advised that you consult a physician before undertaking any new physical training.

Contents

Basic Principles

Thank you for purchasing this book

We at Survive Travel hope it helps you in your amazing journey in Rock Climbing.

The authors at Survive Travel are always creating new publications, and you can get all the latest ones FREE. Simply go to **SurviveTravel.com/Free** and you can get notified whenever they are available free.

Climbing is natural. You knew how to do it as a child and you still know how. Just go out and climb. Use the information here to become better at what you already know how to do.

Holds are what you place your feet and hands onto to climb. They are what you 'hold' onto.

Climb with Your Legs

Your legs are what climb and hold your body up most of the time. Your arms are primarily for keeping balance.

Move your feet up the wall first and use your legs to push you up.

Know where you will place your foot before moving it.

Place your foot carefully and firmly.

Use the edges of your feet or the ball of your big toe.

Press your foot firmly downwards and into the wall.

Trust that you can stand.

Plan Your Route

Plan your route before you start climbing and at least one move ahead whilst climbing. Adjust your plan as needed as you are climbing.

Climb Smooth

Climb smooth and fluid. Don't pause between moves.

Breathe.

Step lightly and only reach as much as needed to grab the hold.

Grip only as hard as you need to.

Gaining Reach

Reach Backwards

Turn away from the hold and reach backwards for it.

It is similar to reaching for something far under a bed.

Stand Up

Stand straight and keep your hips close to the wall with you weight over your feet, as opposed to leaning against the rock.

Bumping

Gain momentum off one hold in order to reach a better one.

Holds and Grips

Edges

A horizontal hold with an edge you can grab onto.

Often flat but sometimes has a lip which you can pull on.

Crimp Grip

Crimping is grabbing the edge with your fingertips flat and your fingers arched above the tips.

Crimping too hard can cause tendon damage.

Full Crimp

To do the **Full Crimp,** place the pads of your fingertips on an edge and curl your fingers so that the second joint is sharply flexed.

Press your thumb on top of the index finger's fingernail to secure the grip.

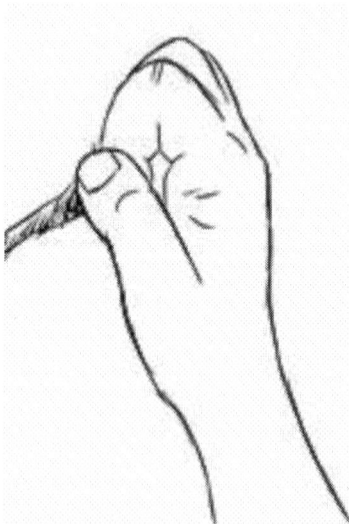

Half Crimp

If you let your thumb press against the side of your index finger, you are using the **Half Crimp.**

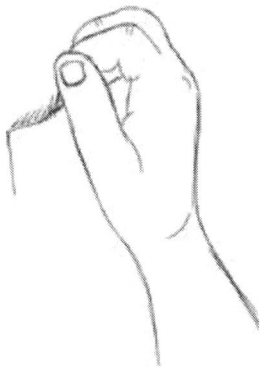

The half crimp is weaker, but less damaging to your fingers. If you have the option, use the Half Crimp.

Slopers

Slopers are rounded handholds without an edge.

They are easiest to grab if they are above you.

Keep your arms straight for maximum leverage when gripping them.

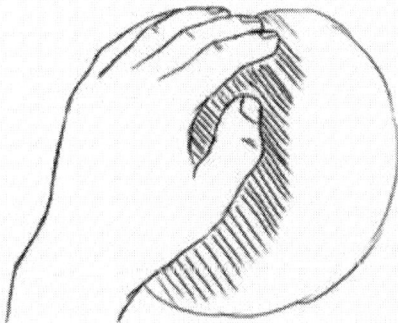

Open Hand Grip

Slopers are used with the open hand grip.

They require the friction of your skin against the rock surface.

Feel around with your fingers to find grip spots.

Wrap your hand onto the hold with your fingers close together.

Feel around with your thumb to see if there is a bump that you can press against.

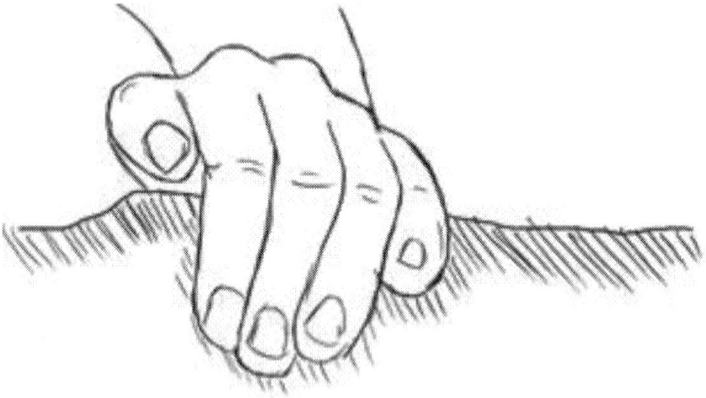

Pinches

Pinches are holds which can be gripped by pinching with your fingers on one side and your thumb opposed on the other.

If the pinch hold is small, use your thumb opposed to your index finger with your middle finger stacked on top.

With larger pinch holds, oppose your thumb with all your fingers.

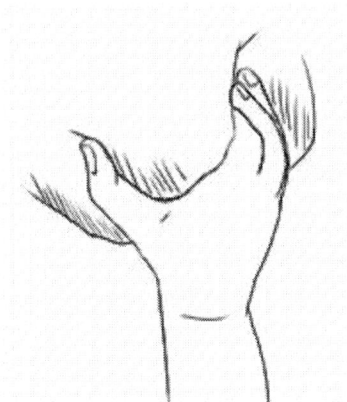

Side Pulls

Side pulls are holds that you pull sideways instead of straight down, due to their orientation.

You can pull outward on the side pull while pushing a foot in the opposite direction to keep you in place.

Pockets

Pockets are holes in the rock surface which you can place your finger(s) in.

Insert as many fingers as you can comfortably fit into a pocket.

Use your strongest fingers first.

Use as many fingers as you can.

Feel inside the pocket to find a surface you can pull against.

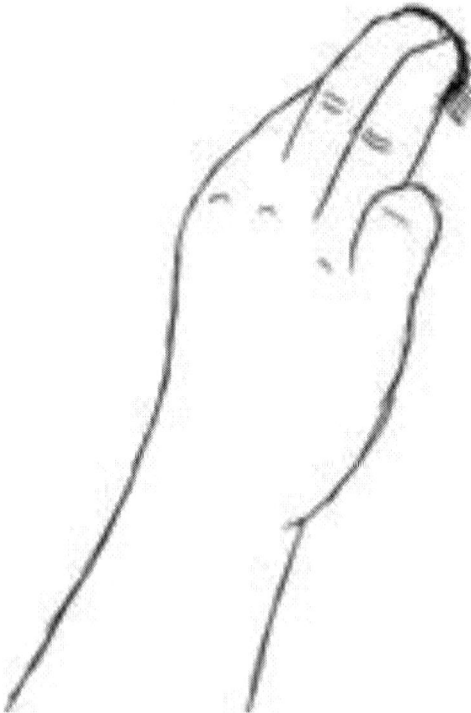

Gastons

A hold oriented either vertically or diagonally and is usually to your front.

Grab it with your fingers and palm facing into the rock and your thumb pointing downward.

Bend your elbow at a sharp angle and point it away from your body.

Crimp your fingers on the edge and pull outward.

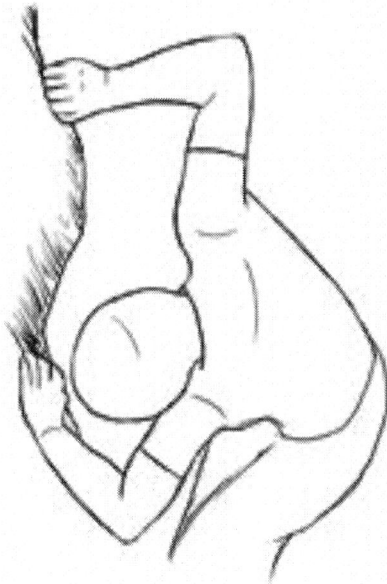

Undercling

Any hold that is gripped on its underside.

It requires body tension and opposition.

Grip the rock with your palm facing up and your thumb pointing out.

Pull out on the undercling and push your feet against the wall.

Palming

If no handhold exists, keep your hand in place by pushing into a dimple in the rock with the heel of your palm.

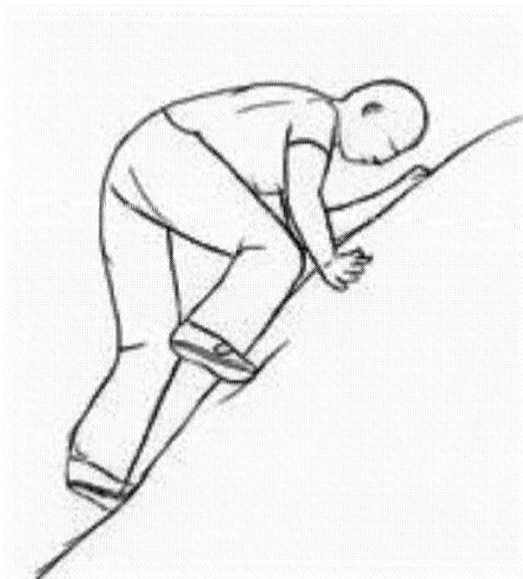

Matching Hands

Matching hands is when you place your hands next to each other on the same hold so you can change hands.

A similar technique can be done with your feet. Do so by slowly replacing the foot and without jumping.

It can also be done with a hand and foot.

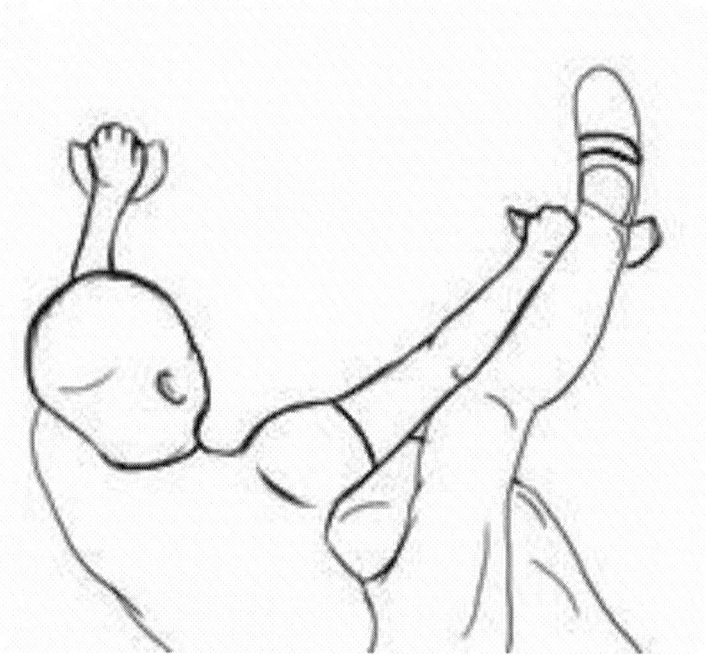

Plan ahead to minimize matching e.g. reach for an extra hold over so your trailing hand can have its own hold.

Foot Techniques

Smearing

Push the flat of your foot hard on the wall, using friction to hold you up.

If you want to go up direct the force slightly downwards.

Return to a foothold as soon as you can.

Back Stepping

Step on a hold so that the outside of your hip faces into the rock, allowing for longer reach in the same direction as the foot that you back stepped.

Drop one knee toward the ground with the other pointing up for an exaggerated back step.

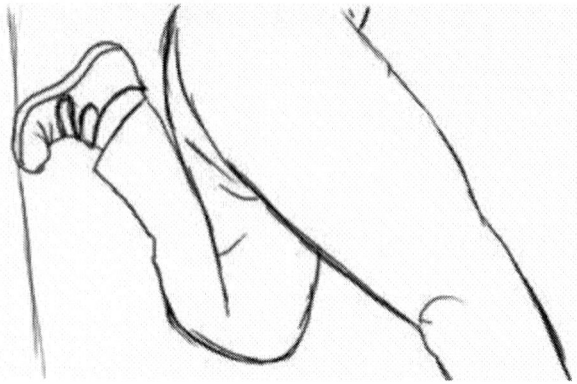

Flagging

Flagging is used to balance your body when reaching for a hold.

Cross one foot behind the other to avoid swinging out from the rock.

Mantle

Use the mantle to climb up onto a ledge.

Get up close to the ledge.

Pull yourself up, rock sideways, turn your hand around and push yourself up until you can place a foot and stand up.

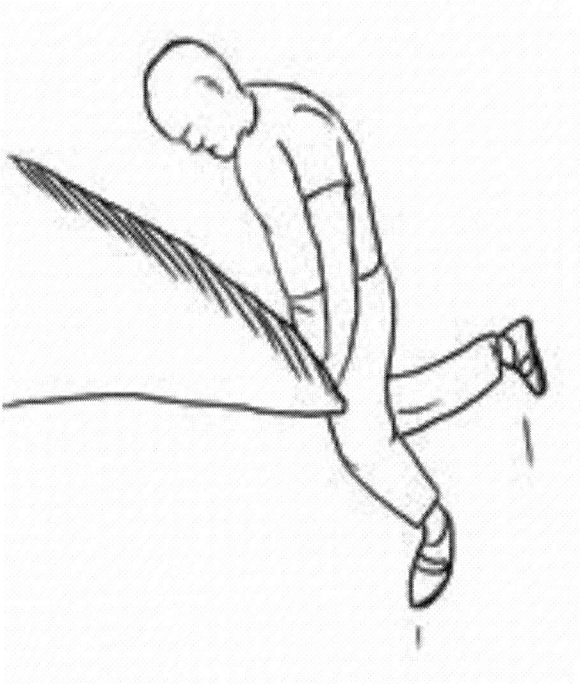

Stemming

Stemming is used to climb opposing walls, otherwise known as chimneys.

Press a foot into one of the walls and your other foot against the other.

Push out with opposing force to hold your weight up.

Do the same with your hands.

Hold your weight with your arms/hands and shift both feet up.

Once you have a good grip with your feet, hold your weight with your legs and move your hands up.

Repeat this 'shuffling' with your hands and feet to climb the chimney.

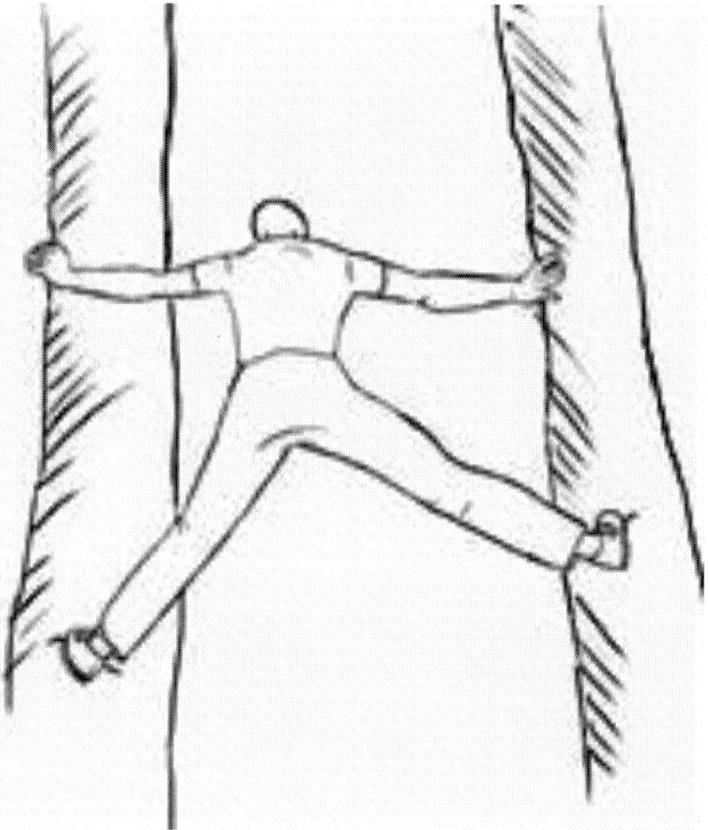

Hooking

Heel and toe hooks can aid in balance and provide leverage for movement.

There are many ways to use the hook e.g. just with your foot to climb onto a ledge.

Hooking under a rock to keep stability whilst negotiating and overhang.

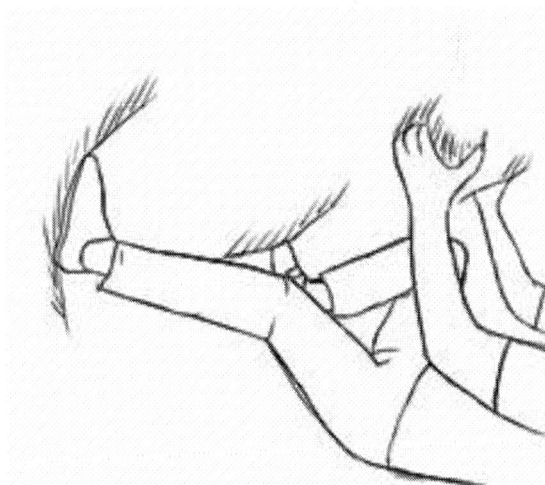

Types of Faces

Slabs

A slab is any rock face than is angled at less than 90 degrees.

Keep your weight centered on your feet.

Stand upright on the rock and away from the slab surface.

Make small steps on small footholds rather than big steps on big holds.

Plan three to five of your intended foot holds ahead at a time.

Aim for big holds and rest when you reach them.

As you climb look for variations in the surface and smear on tiny holds.

Be precise with your toe placement.

Feel the hold with a finger to find the best spot for your foot placement.

Vertical

Vertical faces are angled at 90 degrees i.e. straight up, or near enough.

Keep your weight over your feet as much as possible.

Use an upright body position.

Use your hands and arms for pulling if needed.

Overhangs

Overhangs are rock faces that are overhung or angled more than 90 degrees.

Heel and toe hooks are useful to take the weight off your arms.

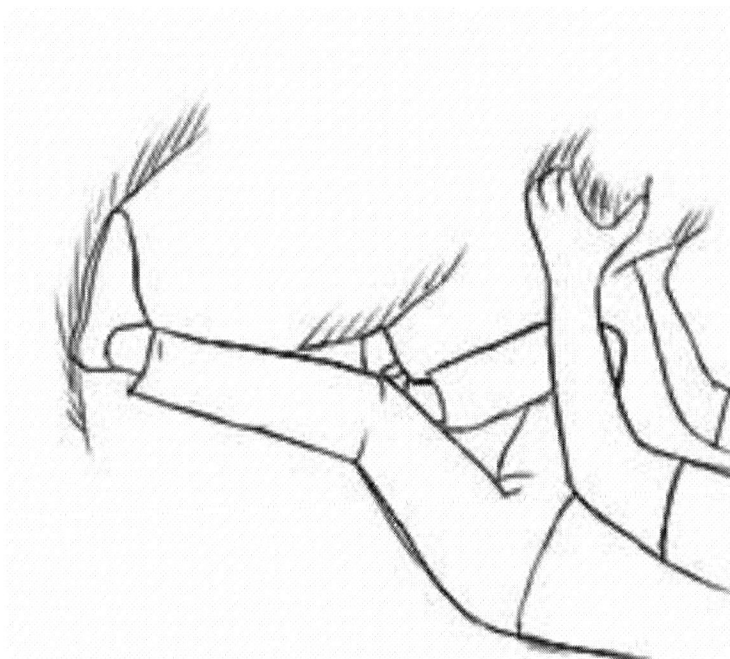

Crack Climbing

Climb the natural cracks in the rock by jamming. Jamming is wedging your body parts into a crack.

Doing so can cut your hands. Prevent this by taping your hands for protection.

Hand Jam

Wedge the side of your hand in the crack with the thumb on top.

Tuck your thumb into the palm of your hand.

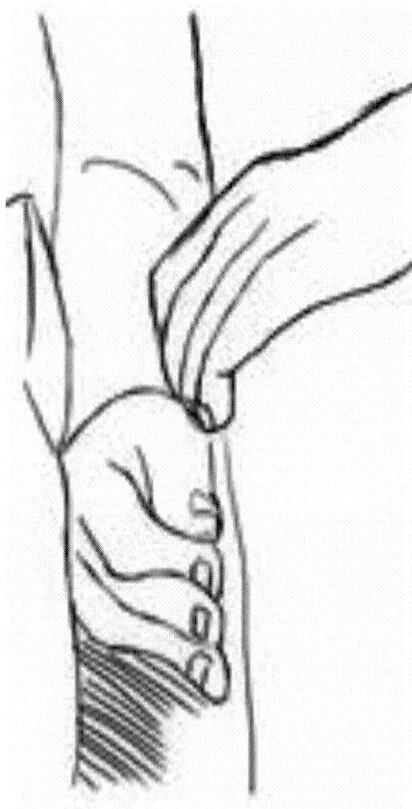

Expand the hand to exert opposing pressure against the walls of the crack.

Hang your weight off your wedged hand.

Foot Jam

Once your hands are jammed into the crack, lift a foot and push the front part of your shoe into the crack.

Stand up on the jammed foot.

Step the other foot up to calf level and jam it in the crack.

Shuffling

Move upward by shuffling your hands up the crack. There are three ways to do this.

➢ Move your top hand up first, then the lower one below it.

➢ Lift the bottom hand out of the crack and hand jam above your upper hand.

➢ Use the above two techniques together.

Do the same with your feet.

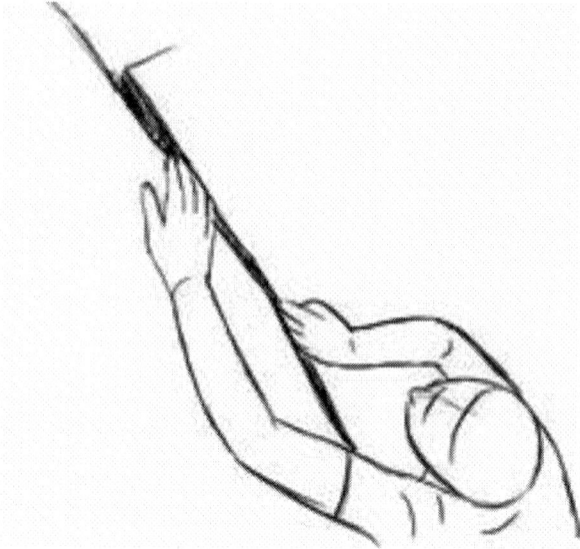

Index

Thank You for Reading

BASIC ROCK CLIMBING

Bouldering, Crack Climbing and General Rock Climbing Techniques

Please visit **SurviveTravel.com/resources** for a bibliography of resources used in writing this book.

If you found the information in this book useful, please let others know by leaving a review from where you purchased it.

If not, you can voice your concerns and/or suggestions directly to the publisher at **SurviveTravel.com/contact.**

Other titles by Sam Fury can be found at

SurviveTravel.com/SamFury

Related Reading

Survival Fitness by Sam Fury

Healthy Living Made Easy, Fast and Cheap by Sam Fury

Available at **SurviveTravel.com/Publications** or wherever you purchased this book

Follow SurviveTravel.com Authors

SurviveTravel.com

Twitter.com/Survive_Travel

Facebook.com/SurviveTravel

Instagram.com/SurviveTravel

Visit **SurviveTravel.com/Free** to get the latest Survive Travel publications **FREE**

10201281R00019

Printed in Great Britain
by Amazon.co.uk, Ltd.,
Marston Gate.